PENGUIN BOOKS
THE ACTOR'S BOOK OF CONTEMPORARY
STAGE MONOLOGUES

NINA SHENGOLD coedited *The Actor's Book of Scenes from New Plays* and *Moving Parts* for Penguin Books. She received the ABC Playwright Award and the L.A. Weekly Award for her play *Homesteaders*, produced by Capital Rep, the Long Wharf, and other regional theaters from Atlanta to Toronto. Her one-acts *Finger Food* and *Women and Shoes*, commissioned by the Actors Theatre of Louisville, have been seen at the Ark Theatre and Manhattan Punchline. Ms. Shengold's translation of Soviet playwright Alexander Galin's *Tonight or Never* was recently produced by Fordham University. She was an executive story editor for the ABC series "Hothouse," has written TV scripts for all three networks, and adapted Jane Smiley's novella *Good Will* for American Playhouse. Ms. Shengold attended Wesleyan University. She lives and gardens in Krumville, New York.